Viral
Marketing
in a week

RICHARD PERRY AND
ANDREW WHITAKER

Hodder & Stoughton

A MEMBER OF THE HODDER HEADLINE GROUP

Acknowledgements

The author and the publisher would like to thank the following for permission to reproduce material in this book.

Circus Restaurant and paybox UK invitation reproduced with the permission of Paybox UK Ltd, Staines, Middlesex.

'What is your No 1 reason for going online?' research data printed with the permission of Forrester Research, Amsterdam, Netherlands.

Time2flirt SMS text message reproduced with the permission of Time2flirt, London.

Every effort has been made to trace and acknowledge ownership of copyright material but if any have been inadvertently overlooked, the publisher will be pleased to make the necessary alterations at the first opportunity.

Orders: please contact Bookpoint Ltd, 130 Milton Park, Abingdon, Oxon OX14 4SB.
Telephone: (44) 01235 827720. Fax: (44) 01235 400454. Lines are open from 9.00–6.00, Monday to Saturday, with a 24 hour message answering service. Email address: orders@bookpoint.co.uk

British Library Cataloguing in Publication Data
A catalogue record for this title is available from The British Library

ISBN 0 340 849045

First published	2002
Impression number	10 9 8 7 6 5 4 3 2 1
Year	2007 2006 2005 2004 2003 2002

Typeset by SX Composing DTP, Rayleigh, Essex.
Printed in Great Britain for Hodder & Stoughton Educational, a division of Hodder Headline Plc, 338 Euston Road, London NW1 3BH by Cox & Wyman Ltd, Reading, Berkshire.

The leading organisation for professional management

As the champion of management, the Chartered Management Institute shapes and supports the managers of tomorrow. By sharing intelligent insights and setting standards in management development, the Institute helps to deliver results in a dynamic world.

Setting and raising standards

The Institute is a nationally accredited organisation, responsible for setting standards in management and recognising excellence through the award of professional qualifications.

Encouraging development, improving performance

The Institute has a vast range of development programmes, qualifications, information resources and career guidance to help managers and their organisations meet new challenges in a fast-changing environment.

Shaping opinion

With in-depth research and regular policy surveys of its 91,000 individual members and 520 corporate members, the Chartered Management Institute has a deep understanding of the key issues. Its view is informed, intelligent and respected.

For more information call 01536 204222 or visit www.managers.org.uk

CONTENTS

Introduction   5

Sunday   Get the basics right   6

Monday   Vital viral ingredients   24

Tuesday   Guiding content principles   36

Wednesday   Host, vehicles and characteristics   45

Thursday   Keep it simple   60

Friday   Start on the right foot   70

Saturday   Get going   86

Dedication

For Amanda and Clare

Thanks to all those people who have supported us in
bringing this book to life. Special reference to the guys at
DS. Emotion, Gyro, Hodder & Stoughton and
the Chartered Management Institute

■ I N T R O D U C T I O N ■

Like everything, the dynamic marketing world never stops changing – evolving constantly with developments that turn yesterday's 'new and improved' into today's 'end of line clearance'. The best products and services manage to evolve with their environment, retaining a constant appeal to their target audience – the best marketers remember those traditional principles and apply them to new opportunities.

For the marketer, this changing world has created a consumer far more informed than ever before. Higher levels of media awareness and even an increase in cynicism towards traditional marketing and selling techniques have certainly created a far more mature, challenging and competitive marketing environment. The sharpest marketers realise that when something new comes along, those that embrace these fresh disciplines and communication routes will have one more tool they can use in their eternal quest for mind and market share.

For the 21st century marketer, one such new discipline is Viral Marketing – a technique which captivates the audience and the marketer alike with its ability to deliver a truly fresh approach to marketing communications.

The opportunity with viral marketing is unique – to use your audience to spread your marketing message, while simultaneously adding their endorsement to it. What is more, they do this instantaneously, to many contacts, with the click of a button.

Over the course of this book you will discover how to plan, implement and measure a successful viral marketing campaign and, therefore, how to embrace one of the most exciting marketing communication developments this generation has seen.

Get the basics right

By the end of today you will know:

- The background to viral marketing and what it is exactly
- Why viral marketing can be so successful
- How viral marketing works and its benefits
- The pitfalls to watch out for

We will start the week by looking at some of the basics behind viral marketing, from what it is and how it works, to why it has become such a powerful communication medium. From here you will be able to appreciate and understand why this relatively new technique is receiving so much attention.

To begin, let us define viral marketing. We do not want to get hung up on lengthy and complex definitions, but it does make for a good starting point. For our purposes viral marketing will be defined as:

> The voluntary spread of an electronic message from one consumer to one or many others, creating exponential and self-perpetuating growth in its exposure.

Over the next 7 days our focus will be to consider viral marketing as the activity of forwarding *electronic messages* from one consumer/user to a number of other people. These electronic messages can take a number of different forms. The most common by far is e-mail.

Viral marketing: an overview

The principles on which viral marketing are based are not new, we have been spreading viruses for years. Think about this:

When was the last time you recommended a good film that you had already seen to a friend?

Or

Have you ever given a friend the telephone number of a good restaurant for an important dinner date?

Things you may have recommended:

- A holiday destination
- A clothing shop
- A restaurant, bar, café
- An airline
- A medical specialist
- A vehicle make or model
- A garage
- A business supplier
- A book, film or music album

These informal suggestions form part of a referral process known as 'Word of Mouth' (WOM) – passing on information to a friend or associate based on your own experience.

A few years ago, before the internet and e-mail came along, viral marketing was being called WOM and in fact, apart from the distribution method, there is not a lot of difference between the two. There are many examples of the latest trend or fashion being spread, not by multi-million pound television advertising campaigns, but rather by individuals simply talking about it, seeing it or hearing about it and creating a ground swell of interest. Think of the phrases, *'I was reading . . .', 'I've just heard . . .'* or *'Have you seen . . . ?'* This is where it starts! Cast your mind back to crazes such as the Rubik's Cube, Cabbage Patch Kids and more recently Micro Scooters, Absinthe and Pokemon – all of these products owe much of their success to WOM marketing. WOM marketing can, when successful, be a marketer's dream ticket; consumers drive brand awareness and product demand themselves.

In many ways the easiest way to understand viral marketing is to consider it as 'super-charged Word of Mouth over the Internet'. I receive a piece of communication from a friend, associate or company, I like what I see so I tell others by forwarding the electronic communication. It all happens at the click of a button, which explains another name for viral marketing; 'Word of Mouse'.

Background to viral marketing?

Viral marketing, as we know, has actually only been around for a few years and only a few savvy marketers have fully taken advantage of its potential. It has become the marketer's latest buzzword, mainly because of some well publisised success stories, such as Hotmail, Levi's Flat Eric and Virgin cinema tickets, to name just a few.

The term viral marketing was first coined by Steve Jurveston of venture capital (VC) firm, Draper Fisher Jurveston. Jurveston and his partners were the venture capitalists behind Hotmail, and it was their idea to add the now infamous tag line *'Get your free, private email at Hotmail'* on to the end of each message. With this, the automatic digital referral process was recognised.

Jurveston initially referred to this process as viral marketing in a 1997 issue of Netscape's newsletter describing the phenomenal success of Hotmail. The term has grown in popularity ever since – Iconocast even gave viral marketing the award for *Internet Buzzword of the Year* in December 1998!

Viral marketing offers marketers an additional weapon in their armoury. On shoestring budgets, successful viral marketing campaigns can increase sales, improve market penetration or market share and enhance brand awareness.

Many of these marketing objectives could be achieved through one traditional marketing communications media such as advertising, direct marketing or PR or through a combination of them. However, viral marketing offers a unique opportunity to supplement (or even replace) these traditional activities with a campaign that offers results at a uniquely low cost, targeting an audience with near-limitless reach.

The wrong sort of virus

This book is about the positive outcomes that can be achieved through viral marketing initiatives, however connotations of the word viral or virus can create all sorts of unpleasant images. Today, the word is also synonymous with computer viruses – bugs that travel around global computer networks in a matter of minutes, often causing havoc and losing millions of pounds in computer downtime. Code Red, Melissa and the Love Bug are just some of the more well-known examples we hope you have not had the misfortune to experience.

Naturally our use of the word viral is about embracing new technologies and using customer advocacy to drive awareness, interest and demand – something all together more positive.

E-mail and viral marketing

The close link between viral marketing and e-mail is obvious and it is important that we realise why, in order to capitalise on potential viral success.

E-mail is the third most popular way for people to communicate, following face to face interaction and the telephone. This popularity stems from a number of advantages the medium can offer:

- Instantaneous written word, both in creation and reply
- One-to-one, or one-to-many communication without the need for physical proximity
- Informality – e-mail has its own language and is becoming ever more relaxed, for example smilies :-) and saddies :-(

The uniqueness of e-mail is the cornerstone of viral marketing success.

Is viral marketing the same as e-mail marketing?

There can be some confusion that viral marketing campaigns are in essence, e-mail campaigns under a different name. This is not true – the host medium provides a key similarity, but that is where the commonality ends. An e-mail campaign can have a viral element if it contains sufficient motivation to forward it on.

E-mail as a communication channel is perfect for the fast dissemination of information, which is a key factor in how viral marketing achieves the results it does. Within e-mail marketing there are many instances where this is not accounted for and opportunities to encourage a viral effect are missed. Below are two examples of e-mail campaigns that have been received in inboxes.

The first example includes a viral element by suggesting that we should recommend a friend and providing a mechanism to enable this, the second includes no such mechanic and does not enable the viral process.

Example one: Circus Restaurant and paybox UK invitation

Dear Richard,

Circus Restaurant and paybox would like to invite you to an exclusive dining experience!

Sign up to paybox and you will be entitled to enjoy a £40 three course evening meal with a complimentary glass of champagne for only £20 by paying with your mobile phone! Any evening from Monday, 19th of November until Friday, 7th of December 2001.

1. Sign up to paybox here
   Please allow two weeks for your application to be processed.

2. Reserve a table
   Telephone Circus Restaurant on (020) 7534 4000 quoting the "special paybox menu".

If you want to invite a friend, partner or colleague, **just forward this invitation**.

Please print out this email and bring it with you as confirmation of the offer.

THE TIMES, October 2001

"perhaps the most innovative and flexible is the recently launched Paybox, backed by Deutsche Bank. The process is almost as fast as handing over cash"

Any questions? Please do not hesitate to contact me.

We wish you a pleasant evening.

Yours sincerely

Elizabeth Cooper

---

paybox uk Ltd :-)))

Consumer hotline 0800 58 729269
http://www.paybox.co.uk
Knyvett House The Causeway, Staines TW18 3BA

The example above features a 'send to a friend' option to encourage referrals, whereas our second example, a standard e-mail, or 'e-shot' as they are often known, has no such referral method.

Example two: MAD.co.uk newsletter

Dear Richard

For top editorial content in your industry, go to mad.co.uk every day for current and reliable news. With content taken from 12 leading industry titles plus a breaking news service throughout the day, mad.co.uk has all the news you need to stay ahead.

mad.co.uk has been first with many stories this month including the inside line on the future of Excite UK and job losses at Cordiant, Circle.com and IPC. Other stories broken by mad.co.uk since the start of August include The Body Shop's campaign against Esso, new account appointments by Jaguar and strategic marketing changes at BT Cellnet, to name but a few. We have also provided up to the minute commentary on the battle between Havas and WPP for control of Tempus.

————————Sponsors Message————————
Think differently about your world, think imaginatively about the challenge you now face, think hard before you choose an agency partner . . . Think!

Redefine your thinking.
http://users.mad.co.uk/advert/default.asp?ad=38&id=21479 –

_____

To subscribe at any level today go to
http://users.mad.co.uk/advert/default.asp?ad=39&id=21479 –

All the team
mad.co.uk

If you do not wish to receive further emails from mad.co.uk please click here

http://users.mad.co.uk/users/nomoremails.asp?usr=21479

Of course, there is a lot more to viral marketing than this, and day by day we shall uncover the key ingredients you should consider.

Key benefits

One of the fundamental elements of successful viral marketing is that messages are forwarded on to friends, family and associates who usually know the sender. The fact that a virus allows marketers to tap into people's existing networks, allowing them to take advantage of the trusting relationships that already exist, does much to explain the power of viral marketing. Who would you take advice from – a nondescript ad, website or brochure, or a personal message sent from a contact in your network of friends, family or associates? Consider when you check your e-mail and you see a mail from a friend. You will always open it, relishing the personal contact just as you would a letter or phone call.

When a recipient chooses to forward any message they have received, they advocate or endorse its content, by associating their name with the message content. In this way, everyone who uses Hotmail becomes a brand advocate every time they send an e-mail, in essence Hotmail's own customers are doing the selling. Trusting relationships and personal affinity are vital to viral marketing – tap into these and watch your virus grow and grow.

These trusting relationships can occur in different strengths and tiers; e-mail creates and sustains secondary friendship levels and you may find yourself communicating with people who, in day-to-day life, you may not have the time or opportunity to keep in touch with. For the viral marketer, these second level contacts greatly increase the size and opportunity for an individual to forward a message.

We can summarise some key benefits of viral marketing:

- The massive adoption of the internet has created an online population of millions, all of whom can be reached with the click of a button
- The speed in which the information travels cannot be matched by any other communication means. Its exponential effect is unique. Within seconds a message can reach countless people, spread all over the world
- The self-perpetuating nature of viral marketing means that the cost per direct contact is minimised. Take the example of Hotmail who, with a budget of only $500,000, attracted over 10 million users in a single year, putting an acquisition cost per user below 5 cents each!

- Viral marketing has a proven correlation between exposure and improved brand recall levels, website usage and customer loyalty unlike traditional techniques like advertising and public relations. This is mainly due to the referral process coming through established trusting relationships
- Viral marketing gives instant credibility to a company or product and is by far the most user-friendly type of marketing. This is driven by the brand advocacy created by sending on the message
- Viral marketing can be measurable, offering the marketer the opportunity to track and analyse how a campaign has performed

Why do we refer?

We all subscribe to referral principles every day – it is human nature to pass on information of value and that has a shared interest. There is a 'feel good factor' in passing on a useful piece of information. For many years WOM has been a favoured marketing mechanic for generating loyal and profitable customer relationships; positive WOM delivers considerable benefits.

Viral marketing is most commonly undertaken for the benefit of the individual 'infected' – the benefit may be educational or entertaining, and whether it is intangible or tangible, the sender believes the recipient will receive gratification from being exposed to the virus.

Natural vs. encouraged

Viral marketing is increasingly a planned marketing activity. However, this is not always the case – even the best marketers do not always recognise what the consumer wants or what they may pick up on. Do you think the team behind Hotmail really expected the phenomenal success they enjoyed? The answer is no – they may have hoped for a strong uptake, but could not have foreseen such a record-shattering outcome.

There are essentially two types of viral marketing. The first covers campaigns that are meticulously planned and agonised over by organisations and creative agencies, such as the recent Spielberg *AI* viral campaign. This example is arguably the most complex viral campaign yet and is rumoured to have cost over $1 million, the most expensive. Revolving around a host of websites identified in the film's trailer, the campaign requires a high level of user involvement and perfectly fits the description of 'encouraged'. Such campaigns are designed specifically with the user's interests and profile in mind.

Secondly there are those that are picked up more naturally, and without such a high degree of planning. Examples could include such things as messages passed between women alerting one another to the dangers of the date rape drug which was widely publicised in America after some women suffered such terrible ordeals. The shared interest (or in this case shared concern) meant that with little planning, the message travelled widely through a viral referral process.

Importantly, this example reinforces research that a bad customer experience will be communicated eight times, compared to a good experience comunicated just once! The natural example epitomises this and is a warning of how a viral campaign can work against you, just as easily as it can work for you.

The viral dimension – how does it work?

So what is the difference between viral marketing and say, advertising or even direct marketing?

When you place an advert in a magazine, its exposure is constant – you will know roughly how many people will see it from circulation figures and readership surveys. The exposure can vary on a number of factors – position, format, and colour – but broadly speaking, the level of exposure is planned to attain a certain level as an integral part of the media schedule. The same applies to a direct mail campaign – if you mail 20,000 contacts you can assume, fairly accurately, that around 20,000 contacts will be exposed to your message.

With viral marketing that level of exposure planning is removed. Initial distribution can be carefully considered (we will examine this further on Friday), and marketers can hope the campaign will take off. However, there is little that can be done to proactively define how many people, in total, will be exposed to the message. Viral marketing is not a science, but more of an art. If you are after accurate forecasting, then use another communication technique. The best you can do to help guarantee success is to follow the ideas and principles we detail in this book.

When successful, through the self-perpetuation of the viral marketing initiative, exposure of the message can reach levels

unparalleled elsewhere in the marketing world. The
exposure patterns of most viral marketing executions show
strong elements of exponential growth. The early phases may
be slow, but as a critical mass is reached, the exposure of the
message increases spectacularly. This exponential trend gives
viral marketing a unique ability to disseminate a message
incredibly fast.

Exponential growth

Tony Blair gets the viral message – fast!

The speed of dissemination of one of the viral
marketing games created for the UK elections in 2001
was carefully monitored by the authors after its launch
two weeks before the country took to the Polls.
'Crouching Tony Hidden Hague', a Street Fighter style
game was launched to a target database of 2000
contacts. Within 24 hours 15,000 different people had
played the game in five continents.

What is more, the feedback loop was closed when a
senior aide to Tony Blair called the game's creators
within six hours to say he would be showing the PM the
game that evening.

The enabler – the growth and acceptance of e-mail

As we mentioned earlier, viral marketing has been enabled
by the growth of the internet and the use of e-mail. Therefore,
it is important to understand how the habits of e-mail use
and penetration have implications for viral success.

We all recognise how prolific the use of e-mail is, most certainly everyone reading this book will have an e-mail account; in fact it is more likely that we will have at least two, one for work use and one for more personal matters.

Number of people online

World total	513.41 million
Africa	4.15 million
Asia/Pacific	149.99 million
Europe	154.63 million
Middle East	4.65 million
Canada & USA	180.68 million
Latin America	25.33 million

Source: Nua Internet Surveys, August 2001

The number of electronic mail boxes around the globe is estimated at a staggering 891 million, with more of them now outside the US than within. In 2000, the number of mail boxes saw a growth figure of 67 per cent from 533 million in use at the end of 1999. What is more, the International Data Corporation (IDC) predicts the number of mail boxes to be around 1.2 billion by 2005.

With so many mail boxes around the world, it is no wonder that the number of e-mails sent on an average day reached 10 billion worldwide by the end of 2001. And there is no end in sight for this growth – by 2005, IDC predicts that over 36 billion e-mails will be sent every day. Our own research, conducted specifically for this book, revealed that 53 per cent of respondents send between 6–20 e-mails per day, while 28 per cent send between 21–50 e-mails per day.

E-mail usage may be considerable but it is also enjoyable. Pew Research, in a recent study, discovered that 70 per cent of e-mail users look forward to checking their e-mail, with 40 per cent saying it is one of the first things they do in the morning, and a further 40 per cent indicating that it is one of the last things they do at night.

'What is your No. 1 reason for going online?'

Research company	No. 1 reason for going on online	% of response
Jupiter Communications	e-mail	92%
Forrester Research	e-mail	89%

Three key observations

- As e-mail volume increases, there will be more e-mail noise and the user may begin to feel overwhelmed, therefore viral marketing success is by no means guaranteed
- People like e-mail; a viral marketer can take advantage of this but should be wary about spoiling someone's enjoyment!
- Understand your customers and how they act and use this intelligence to execute your campaigns

The pitfalls of viral marketing

When you release your virus, you instantly lose control. Only the bravest marketers should attempt it. It is not for the weak hearted – half-baked or weak ideas simply will not work. Be brave and bold.

It is also wise to remember that success is far from guaranteed because referral is such a personal decision. Campaigns that fulfil every success criteria have bombed, whereas campaigns that ignore all the recommendations have seen remarkable success. Viral marketing cannot be controlled and so it is important to think about how you can determine if your campaign has been successful.

Viral marketing is not appropriate for all products and all companies, and many consider it to be limited to larger brands with a focus on youth and fashion. Viral marketing for corporate organisations and those in the business to business sector is more difficult, but there are successes. The trick is not to come across as patronising, desperate or overtly 'salesy'.

Keep it legal

Individuals, not organisations, drive successful viral campaigns. As an individual you do not need your friend's permission to send him or her an e-mail. However, as a professional marketer working on behalf of an organisation, you do need to fulfil a number of legal requirements in the initial dissemination of the message to your target audience.

It is not the Holy Grail . . .

Viral marketing has been deemed by some as the answer to a marketer's prayers – a quick, cheap way to broadcast a message, drive awareness and generate hot leads. Yet, while viral marketing is a powerful marketing tool, it is by no means the panacea that some have made out. The advantages of a viral initiative will become clear over the following pages – as will the pitfalls – and the underlying theme of carefully planned research and targeting will come to the fore.

Summary

Throughout the day, you should have gained a broad understanding of the basic principles and driving forces behind viral marketing. Hopefully you will have begun to see how viral marketing campaigns could be integrated into your own marketing activity. Tomorrow we shall look at how planning is essential for a successful viral marketing initiative.

Vital viral ingredients

Today you will begin to understand the following:

- How planning is as important as execution when creating a successful viral marketing campaign
- The importance of understanding your audience
- Why simplicity is such a critical success factor

A viral marketing campaign needs to be approached in the same way as any other marketing initiative. Considerations like objective setting, targeting and message definition are as important as ever. The basics remain the same, it is only the medium which is new. Today we set out to identify the fundamental planning considerations that need to be included.

Set your objectives

Objective setting encourages you to focus on the results you wish to achieve and helps to ensure a planned and systematic approach to a campaign. Traditionally, marketers have been told that objectives they set should be SMART:

Specific
Measurable
Achievable
Realistic
Timely

This rule still applies when conducting viral activity. Setting objectives at the outset of the campaign allows a marketer to

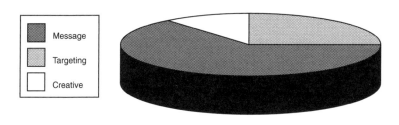

▓	Message
▒	Targeting
□	Creative

ensure that the campaign has been well considered. Once objectives have been established do not file them away – use them to guide the campaign development and if they change, adapt your approach accordingly.

Objectives such as, generating awareness, improving recall levels, building the brand and reaching as many people as possible, tend to be more qualitative in nature and subsequently can be difficult to measure. Try to make these more specific, for example:

- Acquire 1000 new user e-mail addresses
- Generate 5000 new unique visitors to the site

Or even:

- Generate a 10 per cent increase in sales, through cross-selling opportunities

The objectives of a viral campaign do not have to be limited to hits on a website, registrations or new users. The objectives may aim to create a buzz around the brand in order to enhance or change perceptions or create a brand association. The John West Salmon and Budweiser's 'Wassup' campaigns are good examples of this – both are humorous MPEG (Moving Picture Experts Group) movie clips where the entertainment value creates a positive feeling around the brand, thereby stimulating a referral.

Identify your target

By definition, once the virus is released it cannot be controlled and can reach anyone, so you may question the validity of targeting in the first place. However, correct targeting at the beginning is fundamental to success – you need to ensure that the contacts who receive your message, especially those you initially target, have a sufficient interest level in your content. Once the virus begins to be spread by your audience, targeting should occur naturally; those sending it to friends and associates will generally have a good understanding of the characteristics, interests and personality of the recipient. The importance of a *shared interest* is highlighted here as a fundamental element of successful viral programmes.

The stronger the element of shared interest, the stronger your chances of success. A great example of this is Friends Reunited.

www.friendsreunited.co.uk is a website that brings together old school friends all across the UK. The site has captured the imagination of the public to such an extent that its success has become newsworthy in its own right. The coverage generated in the press and radio fuelled the referral process that was already occurring naturally, to a point where some users of the site began placing paid advertisements in local papers to encourage old school friends to register. This almost unique example shows how the power of a good idea and a strong shared interest turns simple referral marketing almost full circle, generating its own PR and promotion.

At the beginning of 2002, Friends Reunited had over 4 million members. For a more in-depth review of Friends Reunited, take a look at the site itself at www.friendsreunited.co.uk.

Understand your target audience

Research is always relevant – try to understand the motivations and profile of your audience. Ask them questions and test your ideas on them, more importantly listen to their feedback. Sometimes the best form of research can be your own gut feeling; the greatest marketers have entrepreneurial characteristics. Balance your own thoughts and beliefs with those of others – either learnt formally through facilitated research, or informally by listening to your colleagues' opinions.

For example, if you are developing a game, get a few people to play it – see how long they play it for, ask them to comment on its playability, and look out for problems with it.

If you are working on an offer to use as an incentive to respond, check that those within your target find it enticing and are interested enough to bother to respond to it. Consider

whether you are going to use a prize draw as an incentive, or whether everyone who replies will receive something.

If you are developing a 'funny' (i.e. a joke or movie) make sure that it is not just you and your colleagues that find it amusing. People's senses of humour can vary considerably and what may be entertaining to one person may well be offensive to another. You need to strike the right balance, without diluting your idea.

This research process is not a one-off activity; it should be encouraged when the virus is alive and this way you will gain a huge amount of real-time intelligence on your target audience. We will cover some practical approaches to tracking on Saturday. If you are using an agency to run your viral campaign, make sure that they have tested their idea and do not forget to ask them if they have executed similar campaigns before and, if so, how they worked.

Audience-centric planning

It is vital to plan your campaign around your audience. It is
no good coming up with a campaign that you think is a
winner, if the people you want to communicate to simply
cannot partake in it.

DVD launch is a little too PC!

When a leading Hollywood studio launched one of its
recent blockbusters on DVD, some very clever
technology was built into the disk. If consumers put the
DVD into a DVD-ROM drive in their computer, they
could access a special website with exclusive trailers
for the film's sequel. That is as long as the consumer
had a PC. If they had a Macintosh, that was too bad.
Mac users couldn't access the special content until a
glitch in the programming had been corrected.

The use of technology as part of an innovative, multi-
channel strategy was excellent, but the lack of planning
and testing caused an embarrassment, highlighting the
importance of thorough testing.

What does audience-centric planning mean?

In short, audience-centric planning is putting the audience
experience at the heart of what you do. When planning any
activity that touches your audience, it is important to
consider how they will react. In larger advertising campaigns
it is often possible to research exactly which campaigns will
be more effective, and in the direct marketing world it is
common practice to test different executions.

In the digital world where it is not as simple to test different executions with the audience, many viral marketers opt for the easy route and plan their viral executions around a lowest common denominator in terms of content, message, level of involvement required or technical usage environment. Yet, while this is one solution to ensure that the campaign is audience-centric, it is not the best way because many powerful, engaging vehicles will be discarded in the hunt for the safe bet. With this in mind, taking the lowest common denominator route is in itself limiting the potency of the campaign.

Through gaining even just a basic understanding of your target audience it is possible to develop some sensible parameters that reflect the level of technical sophistication of your audience.

Take an example – personal e-mail at work

We all do it at work! Send and receive the odd personal e-mail . . . Have a few sneaky minutes checking that Hotmail account . . . So, while it may be an obvious assumption that a business-to-business campaign is likely to land in a working environment, it is also wise to remember that consumers work too.

In fact, according to research undertaken specifically for this book, 79 per cent of e-mails are opened at work. So unless the intention of the campaign is to annoy the user (and yes, some campaigns do aim to do this!), it is worth considering how an informal viral campaign will be received by your audience if they are at work. Sudden loud sounds, for example, could embarrass the user in a quiet office, prompting him or her to click 'quit' followed by 'delete'. That said, as with all audience-centric planning, the skill comes in finding the perfect balance.

What message are you trying to convey?

At the heart of viral marketing is a good idea. From this starting point, the assumption is that the people you send it to will think that it is so good they will pass it on, and so on and so on.

To guide your good idea, try to ensure that you have identified a single-minded proposition or clear single message to convey. Too many times marketers try to communicate multiple messages at one time – focusing on a single message will help to ensure brand recall and avoid any message confusion in the target market (i.e. Hotmail – 'Get your free, private e-mail at http://www.hotmail.com'. Short, simple and single minded).

In the following example the powerful message, once again, is short, simple and single minded.

> **THAMES WATER** have set up a website associated with Water Aid and will donate a total of £150,000 pounds (which will provide safe drinking water for life to 6,000 people in Africa and Asia) if they have 2,000,000 visitors to the site in the next 12 weeks. It only takes a few seconds to visit the site and click on the 'Click Here' message at: http://www.givewater.org/

Check out the competition

Before you release your virus, try to find out if the competition has conducted any similar activity – get yourself on their e-mail listings, see what offers and promotions they are running and how these stack up against yours. Are they targeting the same people as you and are they using the same medium? All this will give you the intelligence to create a campaign that stands out from your competitors.

The continual battle in generating awareness is gaining mindshare, and although viral marketing is great for doing this, you need to remember that more and more people are pursuing this activity. What is more, our survey into e-mail use for this book showed that 55 per cent of respondents received between 6–20 e-mails per day, and a further 26 per cent received between 21–50 e-mails per day. These figures illustrate that e-mail inboxes are becoming as noisy as any glossy magazine filled with ads.

How does the activity integrate with your overall marketing strategy?

Your viral marketing activity must be integrated within your overall marketing strategy and other marketing communications. Campaigns created in isolation will not benefit from wider activity that you may be conducting and vice-versa. We recommend that you do not approach a viral campaign as a quick fix to a problem.

Integration refers to more than simply following corporate guidelines or using the same strap-line. A viral campaign reinforced with other activity will have a greater overall effect. Furthermore, you want to lean over and touch people with your campaign, create a buzz in their workplace and encourage them to discuss it down the pub. When you can achieve this level of online and offline integration, your chances of success are greatly improved.

An example of integration: Metz targets students

A recent campaign into the student community by Metz, the alcopop drink, demonstrated the power of ingenious marketing integration. The campaign leveraged the Metz 'Judderman' character and the unnerving music of the TV ads. The site, at www.spinechillin.com, featured Judderman taking the visitor through his mysterious forest, leading them to a spinning fridge where the visitor entered a competition. This action required the visitor's e-mail address and that of a friend, who subsequently received an e-mail alert. The campaign further integrates with a student's favourite haunt – the student union bar – by using a promotional poster and sticker campaign.

The role of creativity

The use of creativity within any piece of marketing communication can have a significant influence on the overall success of your initiative. Creativity can be defined in a number of ways – from the way you seed or release the virus, to the call to action, to the medium, and obviously to the content itself.

Creativity can determine the success level of your campaign. However, whether your campaign is carried out in-house or by an agency, there is a temptation to make it as unique and creative as possible, sometimes forgetting the message, objective and more importantly the user along the way. Be as creative as you can afford to be, but always remember who you are talking to and what you want them to take from the communication.

The AA encourage the Battle of the Sexes

Motoring organisation the AA extended their recent TV and poster advertising campaign – based on domestic arguments – through the creation of the 'Argumate', a humorous interactive game where the user can test their skills in avoiding arguments and confrontations. The results were collated to determine whether men or women are better at avoiding arguments, building on a battle of the sexes angle which was central to the viral idea. Users could e-mail the game to friends and family, encouraging the viral effect. Visit: www.argu-mate.com.

This example extends the creative platform and creates a fun and interactive dimension to the offline activity. It also demonstrates a good starting point for developing viral executions that integrate creatively with the overall message.

Summary

Today we have looked at some of the key elements you need to consider when developing your viral campaign. Many of these are fundamental to an effective execution and, as with the majority of successful initiatives, the greater the effort spent on planning, the greater the chance of your virus spreading.

Visit www.marketinginspiration.com and you will find a variety of information that will help you with your viral campaign including downloads, useful links and helpful hints.

Guiding content principles

By the end of the day you will have learnt:

- Why content is so critical to a good viral initiative
- The difference between driving sales and building brands in viral campaigns
- How to maximise your chances of engaging with your audience and getting them to drive your viral campaign forward

Today we shall look at the different ways to structure the content and how to make sure that it engages its recipient and ensures its spread. We will also look at some well-known examples to find out how their content underpinned the success they enjoyed.

Great content makes for great viral campaigns

Think of any e-mail you have received recently. Just any message from those in your inbox. The chances are that you are thinking of a message for two reasons – firstly because of who it came from, and secondly because of the content it contained. It may have been a nice message from your partner, or a really good joke from a friend, or one of those movie clips where a skateboarder attempts some impossible trick and it all goes horribly wrong.

You are remembering this e-mail because it has somehow moved or engaged you momentarily. If someone sent you a message with boring or irrelevant content, there would be no reaction. E-mail itself is an empty vehicle – it is the content that makes it a powerful communication tool.

The same basic rules apply to viral marketing initiatives. The most fundamental success criteria for any viral campaign is the content and the personal referral – the make or break factors in getting the campaign to lift off. If you think back to any of the memorable viral campaigns of late – whether it was MTV's 'Stereo MPs' for the election, or Budweiser's 'Wassup' MPEGs, the principle holds true. It is the content that makes the difference between 'forward' and 'delete'!

So why does content reign supreme?

In any marketing activity, it goes without saying that the message to be communicated needs to be planned and researched in order to maximise effectiveness, as we discussed yesterday. In any advertising or direct marketing campaign, the content is one of the key success factors of the initiative and, as such, is mapped out with the greatest care. If the communication fails to engage the recipient, it is simply ignored. The same is true of viral marketing – each and every recipient needs to be engaged by what they receive.

Think about the content when it reaches its tenth round of recipients – people who may not have heard of your company, be familiar with your product or even understand your proposition. Does the content still engage them enough to want to send it on to their friends and colleagues?

Striking a balance between subtle and overt sales messages

The basis behind marketing is increasing demand or raising awareness for your product. Deciding on whether your message will be overtly sales driven or more brand building is a key decision for any viral marketer. If the objective of your campaign is to generate short-term sales and you lead with a sales message, there is a danger that if your offer is not good enough, your virus will die quickly. However, leading with more subtle sales messages contained within an overall branding proposition will help improve long-term sales as well as build your brand. So how do you decide what is right for you?

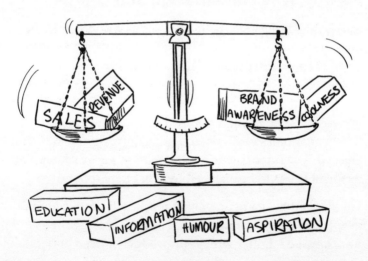

Overt sales
If you have a very strong offer and call to action, you can focus on these in your viral activity, without fear that the virus will not spread. As a consumer, if you are sent a great

offer, you will want to let your friends know about it, just as you would tell them about a great sale on the high street. In the example below, from *The Sunday Times Wine Club*, the offer appears so good that it was forwarded to a select number of contacts – friends who share an interest in wine

---

YOURS FREE – A 12-bottle case of wine normally £70.20!

Dear Mr Whitaker,

From any angle, this is THE best quality wine deal in the UK – 12 bottles of award-winning wine . . . absolutely FREE!

They're serious quality, every one of them . . . like Australian Chardonnay from the World's Best Chardonnay trophy winner, vintage-of-the-decade Bordeaux, a smoothly oak-aged Rioja style and our most scintillating Sauvignon . . .

Simply order The Club's August Highlights mixed case at just £69.99 (plus £4.99 p&p) and receive a Deluxe Dozen of special occasion reds and whites (normally £70.20) – FREE!

Better still, every bottle is backed by The Club's famous guarantee of enjoyment. Don't like them (for whatever reason!), we'll refund you in full, no questions asked.

So give us a try. You've nothing to lose and twelve superb wines to gain. To take full advantage of this once-only offer, and to see the wines, simply go to www.sundaytimeswineclub.co.uk/XA21or call The Club's Express Orderline on **0870 444 7200** (quoting **XA21**).

Best wishes,

Adrian Bentham

Wine Director

The Sunday Times Wine Club

If you would prefer not to receive any further offers from The Sunday Times Wine Club, do please let us know by simply replying to this e-mail, putting the word "unsubscribe" as the subject.

For the viral marketer, the risk with overtly sales-led activity is that without an exceptional offer and call to action, there is no reason for the recipient to spread the virus. Furthermore, an overt sales message can encourage the sender to be more selective – creating a smaller community of more qualified recipients at the expense and risk of limiting the exposure of your message. The quality and not quantity argument speaks for itself here.

Take another example. When a leading cinema chain offered free tickets, the virus spread exceptionally quickly, because the offer was so powerful. However as the offer was limited to 20,000 free tickets and the uptake was so strong, the virus died quickly. Gauging the success of this campaign depends on the cinema chain's objectives – if it was to get 20,000 people to their site and claim a free cinema visit, then yes, it was very successful. If the objective was to build the brand, then the tens of thousands of people who received the virus as it died down and could not get a free ticket would be less favourably inclined to that particular brand.

So what about viral campaigns that build the brand rather than drive sales?

Viral marketing offers an exceptional opportunity to build the brand. Many brands have invested in viral marketing with a focus on the brand; the trick is to ensure that the content is so creative and engaging that it merits passing on to a friend, despite the lack of an explicit offer. Due to the aspirational nature of the 'cool' content, the person forwarding the message becomes part of the 'in crowd'. In essence, the opportunity to be able to impress others through an action is driven by basic human motivations – people like to be liked!

Brand-building campaigns can positively affect your sales figures, but it is likely to be more long term as customers and prospects build an affinity with the brand, have higher levels of recall or recognition and ultimately become predisposed to the product or company.

A good example of this is the recent MTV video clip, created as a viral campaign for Christmas 2001. This spoof piece of home video showed a young boy opening his presents on Christmas day to find that his gift happened to be a genuine, fully functioning Star Wars light sabre. The boy swings the weapon around his head and accidentally decapitates Grandma. Aimed at a specific audience who would see the entertaining side to this movie, the virus reached thousands from a small launch group within just a few days.

This example illustrates that not all campaigns require a specific action, i.e. visiting a website. Some, such as the MTV example, reinforce brand values and create a buzz around the content.

Avoiding apathy

How many times have you received a piece of direct mail containing the latest, greatest offer that frankly you just do not need? And how many times have you thought '*so what*?' before throwing it in the bin? For a direct mail campaign, this kind of reaction can be tolerated – this reaction is even expected from 98 per cent of the recipients, so long as the other 2 per cent think '*that's just what I've been waiting for*' and respond to the campaign. Unfortunately, with viral initiatives this success criteria is not the same.

If a viral campaign is to have sustainable growth, out of every 100 people to receive the virus, we need another 100 referrals – anything less would mean the virus slowly starts to die. If only two people feel sufficiently moved to click the 'forward' button, they will each need to send the mail to 50 people, which is pretty unlikely. If they only sent it to ten people each (i.e. 20 referrals in total) the virus would be in rapid decline. It is important to stimulate a reaction in as many recipients as possible to maximise the number of referrals.

What reaction should your viral campaign prompt from a user? There is no answer to this because the communication objectives of any initiative will be specific, if not unique, to that campaign. Take a charity viral e-mail, for example – here the desired result may well be sympathy and concern or simply awareness of the problem, compared to a Budweiser campaign intended to make people laugh, drive aspirational awareness and reinforce subconscious perceptions that 'Bud' is cool.

While the reactions can be very different, all viral campaigns have a common enemy – *apathy*. Prompting a response – any response – is essential for the campaign to grow. Failing to elicit any response means that the campaign will die because the content fails to move the recipient. That lack of engagement means that the virus will go no further.

Passing the *'What's in it for me?'* test to avoid apathy

It is imperative that the user engages with the content and gets something out of it. This may be tangible (i.e. money off a product) or intangible (i.e. an emotional reaction). If the

content fails to elicit either of these reactions, you will end up with a dead virus. In order to get a positive reaction, your content has to pass what we call the *'What's in it for me?'* test.

Before you go to the effort and expense of developing your viral campaign, there is a simple way to see if you will pass this test. Put yourself in the shoes of the recipient and ask yourself the questions identified below – if you can answer some or all of them positively, your campaign stands a chance of passing the test. If not, you may need to think about the proposed content again.

- Is there a benefit or an offer? Is it compelling enough to make me stop what I'm doing and shout about it to my friends?
- Does it make me look cool/good/educated? In other words, does it position me how I want to be seen?
- Is there a reason for me to pass it on? What is it?

- What would I tell a friend the benefit is? Is it clear to me?
- What will I remember from the campaign? Is there something long lasting?
- How would I convince a sceptic that this is something good?
- What questions or objections would I get from that sceptic, and would I have an answer?
- Could the people I send it to misunderstand something? Is there anything that could make me look bad?

Simply ask your target audience what they would do if they received your virus. Explain how the campaign will work and the response you want from the recipient and ask if this is a reasonable expectation.

Remember that you are relying on your audience to forward the message. They will only forward something if it reflects positively on them, so your content needs to be sympathetic to their preferences. You are in the hands of your audience and you need to keep them at the forefront of your thinking.

Summary

Today we have covered the principles that should guide the direction of your content and how to maximise your chances of creating excellent content. Much of today is theory – tomorrow we shall start to put this into practice.

Viral hosts, vehicles and characteristics

Today, we will cover:

- The different ways your message can reach your audience
- How different content can be applied for maximum advantage
- The three main content characteristics your campaign can adopt

Today we are going to cover the type of virus you will be trying to spread. We can break this down into three areas. Firstly, the host, which is where the virus resides. Secondly, the vehicle by which the message is carried, for example an MPEG movie. And thirdly, the characteristics that are present within this message, for example is it purely for entertainment purposes, or is there an educational element as well?

The host

There are a limited number of hosts for a virus. The two main options are e-mail and a website. This book predominantly relates to these two, but there are a couple more that are worth noting, mainly mobile phone text messages and hand-held devices such as Personal Digital Assistants (PDAs). We will touch on the latter two briefly, later in this section.

E-mail

As people are now very familiar with e-mail, it lends itself well to spreading a virus. When e-mail is the host, the virus is contained within the body of the e-mail, or as an attachment to the message. Although there may be a website or other call to action referenced, the virus can be spread and understood simply by forwarding the e-mail to another person.

The great advantage is that the spread is made easier by simplifying the actions required to become infected, i.e. you do not need to visit a website. The main disadvantage is that there are limitations with the type of content you can spread – such as the size of a file attachment and any special applications that are required to view the content.

HTML or text?

One of the key questions when using e-mail is whether to use a plain text or an HTML (HyperText Markup Language) (an e-mail designed using HTML may contain graphics, rather than a pure text-based e-mail). The basic answer is that both can usually be created within an e-mail (known as a multi-part e-mail) and your e-mail application will detect what it can read. As a rule of thumb, approximately 80 per cent of e-mail users can read HTML e-mails and IMT Strategies reports that as of September 2001, 57 per cent of marketing e-mail received by online users was in HTML format. The type of e-mail you send depends upon your content and your audience.

Websites

Due to their massive adoption, websites make a perfect host for your virus. When a website is the host, the recipient will need to visit the website to be infected and experience the virus.

Many of the issues regarding inclusion of content within the body of an e-mail are avoided if the content is on a website, mainly because the user's environment can be more controlled. For example, games, interactive competitions and large file-size content can sit easily on a website, but spreading these within an e-mail is more difficult. Tracking the virus is also easier when the host is a website – we will cover this more on Saturday. There are again disadvantages that need to be weighed up, a key consideration is that it requires the user to visit the website, adding a further obstacle to the infection process. You will also be placing a large amount of strain on your Web server. Finally, not everyone who has access to e-mail necessarily has access to the Web such as users of interactive TV and restricted Web browsers.

An example of a simple Web-hosted campaign from the NSPCC

```
SUBJECT HEADER: Re: Chariddy . . .

Donate to the NSPCC for free. It'll take
two seconds . . . Just click on this link,
and then the green button to have
Microsoft give the NSPCC 8p on your
behalf. Pass this on to your friends.

http://www.nspcc.org.uk/donate-4-free
```

In this example the recipient is required to visit the website to complete the infection. Without this action the virus is incomplete.

Other hosts

We mentioned that other hosts are available and although far less common than e-mail and websites, text messaging and PDAs are becoming more widely used.

Mobile phones

Short Message Service (SMS) or text messaging can also play host to a viral campaign. This is currently being utilised by a limited number of companies. As with any new technique, success levels vary and much depends upon the content of the message. Initial indications suggest that SMS as a viral vehicle is more likely to be successful in the youth or younger professional market places.

Example: Time2flirt mobile phone campaign

The above example to promote a London club night used simple text to convey the message. SMS is more limited than e-mail and websites hosts. Text-based messages are the most popular, however ring tones and phone logos are other examples of viral elements that can be transmitted to mobile phones.

Personal Digital Assistants (PDAs)

PDAs can also be used to host a virus. These small hand-held devices are becoming ever more widespread and many applications (usually free downloads) are spread using this method.

If the content is rich enough and it is free, then a viral effect can be created. The virus is usually a 'natural' spread and tends not to be actively encouraged by the content originator.

Which one is best for you?

It is impossible to specify the single best host because the choice must depend on the campaign and its objectives. What we can say is, stick to what you know and if it is a good idea it will spread. You will probably get more success from e-mail and websites than using other hosts.

The vehicles

The viral vehicles are wide and varied. Below some of the vehicles are listed that you may have received. The vehicle is not particularly important within itself; you can use any of them to convey your message and build the viral effect.

Examples of viral vehicles

Jokes
Stories
Tests, e.g. personality tests
Trivia questions
Warnings and spoofs
Still images
Sound files
Movies
Competitions
Incentives and offers
Games

We have investigated some of the limiting factors that will affect the use of the vehicle and you will find out more about these on Thursday.

Quick reference guide to attachments

You may be sending out content attached to an e-mail. If so, here is a simple guide to the types of file you could be sending, the file format, and the plug-in a user will need in order to view the content you are sending.

Content type	File format	Plug-in/Software
Movie file	MPEG (.mpg) QuickTime (.mov) AVI (.avi)	Windows Media Player QuickTime Player
Static image	JPEG (.jpg) GIF (.gif) TIFF (.tif) BITMAP (.bmp)	Graphic package or Web browser
Sound file	WAV (.wav) MP3 (.mp3)	Sound card and player
Program	Executable (.exe) Projector	No software – just need PC for .exe or Mac for projector
Moving Web graphics	Flash movie (.swf)	Flash Player
Uneditable document	PDF (.pdf)	Adobe Reader
Text document	.doc .txt .rtf	Microsoft Word or Text editor
Spreadsheet	.xls	Microsoft Excel
Web page	.htm	Browser
Compressed file	.zip	WinZip Stuff-it Expander
PowerPoint	Slide show (.pps) Presentation (.ppt)	Microsoft PowerPoint

Which type of vehicle is best for you?

As recognised all along, much depends upon the type of campaign you are promoting and, indeed, the budget that you have available. If you are working on a low budget campaign, the chances are that you cannot afford to go and shoot a movie clip – however, you might be able to produce a research document that your audience will find valuable. When you have set your objectives and got to grips with your audience, the choice of vehicle will become more obvious.

For your reference, here is a table based on research for this book. It shows how likely recipients are to forward on a particular vehicle. This is only a rough indication – the reality will be more determined by the potency of the specific content.

(Please note that in our survey we asked respondents to rate the likelihood of forwarding a message on a scale of 1 to 5, with 1 being unlikely and 5 being very likely to forward.)

Unlikely 1 – 5 likely	1	2	3	4	5
A joke or funnny story	9%	19%	23%	25%	24%
An incentivised competition	16%	31%	21%	17%	15%
An education message	21%	33%	28%	12%	6%
An amusing movie/ image/sound file	19%	21%	23%	28%	9%
A work-related document	12%	14%	15%	34%	25%
A game	27%	23%	22%	20%	8%

The characteristics

OK, so we know about the types of host and viral vehicle, now it is time to look a little more deeply at the fundamental characteristics of what makes viral content so contagious. All successful campaigns – in fact all communication – aims to stimulate an emotional response. But viral marketing has a twist – as viral marketers we need to create an emotional response which will in turn motivate the recipient to continue the spread of the message.

We have identified three main categories Entertaining, Educational and Rewarding – viral campaigns will fall into one of these. However, they are by no means mutually exclusive – in fact if your campaign can feature two or all of the characteristics, your chances of success will increase.

Entertaining

The most popular and, arguably, the most successful type of viral activity has an entertaining value. If you think about the type of content that you have personally spread, the chances are that entertainment is pretty high on the list.

We usually associate this with amusing content – whether it

is a straight joke or amusing movie clip. Some of the well-known viral examples can be classified as entertaining, for example Levi's' Flat Eric and Budweiser's 'Wassup' initiatives. Here the sender has a feeling of 'coolness' by being associated with the content of the message.

So how do you apply entertaining content to your own campaign?

If you are going to follow this option, your primary objective should have a brand-building focus and not a sales-led one. Therefore, you need to ensure that your message is not overtly sales focused, but more subtle in nature.

For example, when Flat Eric was initially released by its PR and advertising agencies there was no reference whatsoever to Levi's. It was only when the viral campaign officially launched to coincide with the ad campaign that the Levi's brand was promoted. Before the official launch, this piece of unbranded viral marketing had seen prolific growth, purely because its content was so innovative, cool and entertaining. It was only when the advertising campaign broke that any brand association was made, thereby exploiting the mass awareness already generated.

The core objective in Levi's campaign was to raise awareness of the new product and regenerate the flagging Levi brand. By association, if this was successful there would be an increased demand and subsequent revenue generation, which ultimately there was.

Such examples illustrate how the user can discover the brand for themselves, and it gains acceptance and familiarity, rather than having a brand or sales message forced on to them which can alienate and encourage non-acceptance.

It may go without saying, but you need to make sure that your content is actually entertaining – Levi's used one of the best advertising agencies in the business and they got their result – outstanding, award-winning, creative. You do not necessarily need to have a huge budget, however, you do need to have a good idea.

Educational

Most commonly, educational content is spread to a more select group of recipients, purely because it does not have such a broad appeal as entertaining content. Shared interests, which define how far a virus will spread at each referral, are likely to be more specific in this scenario. Think of a free piece of research you find on the internet – you are unlikely to send this out to the entire company, but you may well send it on to your project team or boss, if it relates to the work you are currently undertaking.

Alternatively, imagine that you are on the Web, checking out your stock portfolio and notice some top tips on some potential purchases; you remember some friends who might find these useful and send the information to them. You have just taken part in your own educational viral campaign, created and executed by yourself. The chances are your usage of this site will increase, as will your loyalty as a result of your action.

That said, educational content could also have a very broad appeal – take the example of a charity viral campaign, which serves to alert the population of a problem such as water shortage in developing countries. Such an issue has a wide shared interest and, therefore, a larger potential audience.

So how do you apply educational content to your own campaign?

Content with educational characteristics is particularly flexible because it can be applied to campaigns with either brand-centric or sales-centric objectives. The nature of the educational message will, as ever, depend upon your target audience and what they find interesting or relevant.

Educational content is a good choice for improving positive associations, while raising awareness and building the brand. It can work particularly well in business-to-business campaigns, where valuable information can be used to propel the virus. Often this information is already within the knowledge pool of the organisation and simply requires a campaign to be wrapped around it.

Rewarding

The third characteristic of contagious viral marketing is rewarding, or perhaps more accurately, a direct, tangible reward. This usually manifests itself in the form of incentives, time-limited offers, promotions or competitions. They are the most blatant types of response-driven viral marketing and most appropriate when short-term demand generation is the primary objective.

Reward-focused viral marketing campaigns will contain a direct and personal benefit to the recipient. Any company can create a rewarding campaign, whereas some may find it more difficult to create an educational or entertaining execution. In business-to-consumer marketing, the reward is usually aligned to the individual, or in a business-to-business context, the reward may focus on the company or both the company and individual. For example, if you order a specific type of product, there could be money off (a benefit for the company) together with a free gift (for the individual).

Central to the success of a reward-based viral content is the need to ensure that the reward is appealing to the target audience. The *Sunday Times Wine Club* example identified yesterday is a great example of a simple direct response e-mail that has gone viral. Why? Because the offer was strong for this shared interest group. The plain text e-mail execution was simple and the offer was a winner.

Online retailer forces the issue . . .

In June 2000, an online wine retailer sailed very close to the wind with a viral initiative to boost their UK customer base.

The viral vehicle was a competition to win a group holiday for the entrant and four friends, whose e-mail addresses had to be specified. These friends all then received an e-mail from the company explaining that they had been nominated for the competition by their friend, but that the group's entries would be invalid if they did not confirm their entry for the competition, thereby registering for the site.

Understandably many of the 'friends' were alienated by the dot-com company, as they felt the company had been put under pressure to register, so as to avoid letting their friends down. Clearly these people would not be favourably inclined to that particular brand after that, even if they did enjoy the odd tipple!

So how does rewarding content fit into your own campaign?
Reward-based content can offer a simple route to viral success. If the offer is compelling enough, it will engage the user and spread amongst the shared interest group.

With this type of content it is essential to identify what response you want from the reward you are offering. In some cases this is very simple, such as a 'Buy-one-get-one-free' offer. In other cases the response could be to click on a website, enter a competition, request information, trial a new product or make an appointment. Once you know what you want your recipients to do, the all-important call to action can be developed. As always, keep it simple and clear and you will enjoy a greater level of success.

As this type of content is so focused on generating a response, it is most commonly applied in campaigns intended to drive revenue rather than build the brand. Although, as we mentioned yesterday, both of these objectives have an indirect effect on one another. In this sense, a good offer that spreads around the internet like wildfire will not only drive revenue and uptake, but will also build brand awareness.

Summary

Today we have looked at how to give your viral idea the right host and vehicle, while also considering the most appropriate characteristics to help ensure viral success. Tomorrow we shall look at some of the pitfalls to avoid when creating your virus.

Keep it simple

By this evening you will understand:

- The factors that can limit the success of your viral campaign
- How technology can get the better of you if you are not careful
- Key factors to consider regarding where your content should reside – i.e. on a website or in the e-mail itself

It goes without saying that in any marketing activity, there are numerous ways for a campaign to go wrong, which can greatly limit the success the campaign would otherwise enjoy. All of these limiters can be applied to viral marketing campaigns as much as to traditional media, however the viral campaign has an added dimension – technology. With content viewed and passed on through connected electronic devices, the technical platform provides yet another area where mistakes can be made, and the success of the campaign can be restricted. As marketers are familiar with the limiting factors offline, the focus of today will be to shed light on these new technology-based success limiters.

Do not let technology get the better of you

As previously identified, the most common way to limit the success of a campaign is by alienating or omitting potential users, and technology is very good at doing just this. However, many of the key technical limiters (identified below) can be removed through careful planning. The factors are split into two lists, representing the two basic 'host' environments discussed yesterday, namely e-mail and websites.

Limiting factors for content within an e-mail

Speed: 79 per cent of people who can, will pick up their e-mail at work. For these people, who usually have the luxury of a fast network connection, speed is not often a major concern (although waiting even a short time can be frustrating). Nevertheless, most people connecting to e-mail away from a work environment do so on a 56k modem (in other words a modem that – in theory – transfers 56 kilobytes of data per second. In reality however the data transfer rate is likely to be just one-third of this). And so, one of the main success limiters for e-mail-based viral campaigns is speed. With a large attachment included, the e-mail may take a long time to download, frustrating the user even before they have seen its content.

The table below displays the research conducted specifically for this book about how long people are prepared to wait for files to open.

Time allowed before quitting	Percentage of respondents
Less than 30 seconds	21%
30 seconds to 1 minute	48%
1 to 2 minutes	19%
2 to 3 minutes	11%
More than 3 minutes	1%

As you can see, if the time to open the file is more than 1 minute, then you will have lost nearly three quarters of your audience.

If your audience is likely to have a large proportion of home users with slower connection speeds, the effect of file size becomes very important. A typical attachment of 100k would take a few seconds to come through, however a movie file of a couple of megabytes could take nearer 2 minutes. With users paying for a telephone call to their service provider, this can understandably be very annoying. On top of this, files in excess of 2 megabytes may crash the connection altogether! When this happens, the chances are that the user will not try to pick up the message again, stopping the virus in its tracks.

With this in mind, the first rule for attachments is a simple one – the smaller the better. Failing this, think about optimisation – this technique can help reduce file sizes in the majority of cases.

Large file attachments can also cause significant issues if you are launching your virus internally i.e. if a number of people are sending the e-mail at the same time it may crash your own web server.

Firewalls: more and more confidential information is passed via e-mail and the potential for security breaches is very high. As a measure to safeguard a company's material against dangerous computer viruses (such as Melissa or the Love Bug) or against hackers, many larger companies implement a firewall which acts as a security fence, screening who and what can pass into the company's IT environment. What is more, as e-mail – and internet usage is now so prevalent in today's working environment, many companies are using their firewalls to help stop abuse of the IT infrastructure. In an increasing number of companies, viewing certain types of content, such as pornography or pure entertainment, is not permitted. The firewall can examine content and it may be applied as a filter to ban such unsuitable content.

While implementing a firewall is undoubtedly a very sensible move for the organisation, it does have an implication on the viral marketer looking to spread a campaign through an e-mail attachment. Often certain file types will not be allowed through the firewall, either because their content will be deemed unsuitable or due to the possibility of transmitting a dangerous computer virus. The most commonly refused files are video files (such as MPEG or AVI) and executable files (self-running files) such as the .exe files for a PC or Mac program files. If your content is in this format, spreading it by an e-mail attachment may not be the most effective method.

Plug-ins: from your audience-centric planning you should know the level of sophistication of your audience. Remember this when you come to choose the host and vehicle for your campaign; it is easy to create a campaign that takes advantage of technology that your audience does not have.

Using functionality like Macromedia Flash can make your content more dynamic and engaging, but if the audience does not have the Flash player plug-in (an additional piece of software that can be downloaded from the internet) they will not be able to see the content at all. Even the specific version of the plug-in can cause problems. There are no hard and fast rules to follow. You need to choose a sensible compromise that will suit your audience without compromising your campaign.

Platform: do you work on a PC or a Mac? Or even a UNIX machine? It is an important question to ensure your campaign is open to the widest target audience. The platforms are increasingly inter-operable (in other words, they talk to each other much better!). However, there are still some inconsistencies which may mean that the content you have included in your e-mail attachment will not work on a particular machine. The most common by far is an .exe file. Although these are great for PC users because they require no other software to run, for Macintosh users they are simply a waste of time – they cannot be used. The reverse is also true – a Mac program file (which does the same job as the .exe file) will be useless to a PC user. Other examples exist, but the underlying rule is a simple one: test it. Try to run your campaign on as many machines as possible, from Macs to PCs and UNIX machines, and from the oldest to the newest. This is the best way to identify any problems before your users tell you about them!

E-mail application: as with any software application, there are many variants and versions of e-mail application. However, unlike, for example, a word processing application, with e-mail there are now two very distinct methods to access messages.

1 Through a typical desktop application such as Microsoft Outlook, Quick Mail or Lotus Notes

2 Through a Web-hosted interface such as Hotmail

The main difference is that by definition, the Web-hosted e-mail systems show content as a Web page, so sending out an HTML mail will not cause any problems because HTML is the language used for the creation of web pages. The vast majority of desktop applications will also be able to display an HTML e-mail. In some of the older desktop applications, however, HTML can cause a problem, resulting in the message content turning into line after line of meaningless code.

The prevalence of these old desktop applications is reducing all the time and, as HTML e-mails are now so common, users of these applications will usually know the problem when they see it – and will often be resigned to the fact that their application is rather out of date. That said, it is something that can limit the effectiveness of your campaign and, as such, deserves a mention in this section. With this in mind, the rule is simply to be aware of the problem. If you feel there is a likelihood that your audience may have some old software, plan the campaign accordingly, eradicating the use of HTML in the e-mail message. Alternatively, incorporate a multi-part e-mail that will detect whether the e-mail application can support HTML, if it can not, it will show a text only version.

Limiting factors for content hosted on a website

Speed: this is still an issue for viral campaigns where content is hosted on a website. Users are increasingly used to Web pages which load quickly, so long loading times will have the same effect as slow downloads on e-mail campaigns. Keeping file sizes to a minimum will give a faster file transfer time and using techniques such as streaming for movie clips (which allows the movie to begin playing the early parts while the latter stages are still downloading) will help get your content in front of a user more quickly. Also remember to include a loading progress bar for big or slow files – a user will be more likely to wait if they can see how much time is needed for the content to appear.

Browser version: just as e-mail applications vary, so do browsers (the interface through which a user views a Web page). Similar to e-mail applications, the same basic rules apply. If you are hosting content on a website, check it works on as many browsers as possible, from the latest and greatest to older, less advanced versions. Functionality changes with each new release, so make certain that your content can be viewed effectively on a browser version typical within your target audience, not just on the very latest version. If you are working with a marketing or new media agency, ask them to advise you on this, and check with them that they will design the Web pages to work effectively on the two main choices: Microsoft's Internet Explorer and Netscape's Navigator.

Plug-ins: as with content attached to an e-mail, web-hosted content may require a plug-in. The same rationale applies –

make sure your campaign is accessible to your target audience by understanding their technology environment. There is no point in creating a campaign using the features from the latest Flash 5 version, if the majority of your audience only have the more common Flash 4 on their machines; these people will be unable to see the content. Achieving that all-important compromise is vital.

Corporate policy: previously mentioned in the section above on firewalls, many companies have strict policies on internet usage. With 79 per cent of e-mails accessed from a work environment, it is important to consider the effect this can have. For the viral marketer it is an uneasy position – on the one hand trying to respect these policies, yet on the other hand trying to create a campaign which is extremely engaging and by its nature will distract the user from what he or she should be doing. Again, this is an example of where the viral marketer must find a balance.

Functionality: one common limiting factor that is easy to address is the usability of Web-hosted content. The obvious rule to heed is to keep it simple. No matter how Web-savvy the audience, the easier you can make it, the better. Keep the number of clicks (how many links a user has to follow to reach the desired content) to a minimum – any more than three clicks and there will be a drop off in users.

It is also wise to develop the functionality of the site around the guidelines specified by the World Wide Web Consortium. These guidelines, while not legal requirements, do set out a framework for good practice for the functionality of a website, ensuring the site works effectively for as many people as possible, in particular those with special needs. You can check out these guidelines by visiting www.w3.org

or following the direct link to the latest guidelines from
www.marketinginspiration.com.

A final limiting factor for Web-hosted content is the vital
issue of *scalability*. If a campaign does take off and the site
receives a high number of visitors, the last thing a viral
marketer wants is the site to crash due to heavy traffic levels.
Scalability, as a technical element of a viral marketing
initiative, is examined in more detail on the
marketinginspiration.com website.

Making Web-hosted content run smoothly, with a little help from your friends

When it comes to technology, marketing professionals often
are not the best people to understand and implement robust
IT architectures that will deliver the perfect platform for a
Web-based viral marketing campaign. So, call in the experts –
for those with the luxury of an in-house IT resource, involve
representatives in your campaign. If you work with an
agency, pass the technical bit over to them. For those lone
rangers tackling the campaign alone, speak to your Internet
Service Provider about your objectives. Once aware of these,
your technical support will help to ensure that the technical
platform achieves them.

Although, the focus of this book is firmly on viral marketing
and not on technology architectures, we have included a
section in the www.marketinginspiration.com website to
help your conversations with the technical team. This
highlights the questions to ask and gives some tips learnt
from experience. Specifically, this section of the site covers

optimisation, load testing and scalability – all essential technological considerations for a successful viral initiative.

Summary

Today we have looked at the factors that can limit the success of your viral marketing initiative and the actions that you can take to minimise their effect. It has been quite a technical day, but hopefully you have gained a new understanding of a key difference between viral marketing and traditional word of mouth – the technology involved in distribution. As well as this, do not forget the basics, like targeting, the proposition and naturally the strength of the idea in the first place – these will all have an impact regardless of any technology issues. Tomorrow we will look at the ways that you can launch your virus.

Start on the right foot

Today, you will learn:

- How to successfully launch your campaign using direct and indirect launch pads
- How to sustain your viral campaign over time
- There are different types of recipient of a viral message and how this can affect success levels

After learning how technology can limit the success of a viral campaign yesterday, we will spend today examining the options available to launch and sustain a viral marketing initiative. We shall look at the importance of timing, before finishing with an overview of how people react to a viral campaign, and the difference that this can make to their propensity to pass on your message to their network of friends and associates.

Getting your virus out there

There are a variety of ways that a virus can be launched into a target community, together with a number of ways to ensure that the life of the virus is sustained.

Many critics of viral marketing cite the fact that the medium involves a lack of targeting control and that this is its biggest weakness. However as already mentioned, the campaign will only pass between individuals where there is a shared interest in the content; this acts as a natural filter to keep the virus broadly within its target audience. Therefore, arguably, using personal relationships and networks as your targeting method is more effective than a purchased data list, where targeting assumptions are based on mass profiling information. With this in mind, viral marketers can counter this criticism with the knowledge that this self-selection acts as a natural targeting mechanism.

Self-selection does of course mean that you can expect a degree of fall out from the initial launch – do not worry about this, a certain amount of natural filtering is inevitable even if you have followed the principles discussed earlier in the week.

The viral process

The following diagram below shows what happens when someone receives a piece of viral marketing. Ideally that person will receive the communication, take a look at it, be engaged in some way and decide to forward the message on. However, at any stage the virus can be dismissed: a user could fail to (or be unable to) open the communication; take a look but not be interested or engaged; find the content engaging, but simply decide not to forward the message on. All of these reactions mean that the virus has died for that person.

This illustration highlights just how important the content of your campaign is – if the content is poor or the characteristic(s) inappropriate, a larger percentage of the recipients will not be engaged and will dismiss the campaign rather than send it on.

Content engagement process

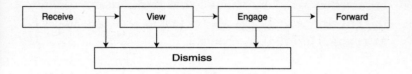

Viral marketing launch pads

The following chart details the main options for launching your campaign. Remember that the launch of your virus can be staged, allowing the spread of the campaign to be orchestrated over a period of time throughout a wide community – this may have the advantage of avoiding a quick peak and subsequent quick death of the virus.

The launch can use one some or all of the methods identified. The choice depends very much on the target audience, as well as on time and budget. The simple fact underpinning this is that the more launch pads that can be built into the campaign, the better.

It is wise to remember that the launch process is critical to success and, in fact, is the only stage within a live viral campaign that can be controlled. Once you set the campaign free, it lives or dies at the hands of the recipient.

Once launched, a good virus will spread itself. So how do you get the campaign to the inboxes of people who will pass it on?

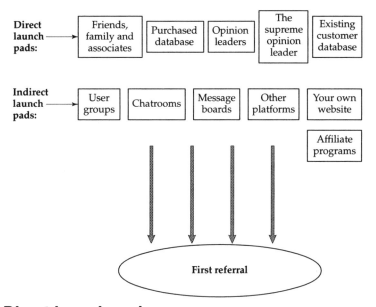

Direct launch pads

These offer a direct communication channel to the recipient –
in nearly all instances this occurs through the use of e-mail.
This method is used predominantly to launch the viral
campaign, rather than to offer an ongoing method to sustain
the referral process. In this sense direct launch pads offer a
short 'blast' of high volume referral in place of the steady
stream created by the indirect launch pads.

Friends, family and associates
One of the simplest and best ways to launch a viral marketing
initiative is to use your existing network of friends, family and
associates. As we have identified, viral marketing relies on the
relationship and trust between the sender and recipient, so
using your own network allows the first step of the process to
be taken within an environment where that trust is strongest.

Numbers may be small from this launch pad, but by asking people in your organisation, your friends, family and associates to launch the virus, a strong initial push can be created.

Naturally, targeting is still important within this audience – sending your retired parents a campaign about 18–30 holidays is unlikely to impress them! It is important to select those contacts that still fall within your target audience.

Purchased databases

Lists of e-mail addresses can be readily purchased, with all manner of databases available. When working with a purchased list, it is important to stay within legal and ethical requirements. Make sure that the list you buy is permission based (in other words the contacts on the lists have given their permission to be included on the database). Also ensure that the list is opt-in (referring to the contact having actively requested to be sent information from third parties, rather than simply *not having specified* that they do not want to receive any third party communication, know as an opt-out list). Visit the website at www.marketinginspiration.com for links to sites where you can request a free summary of these important laws.

The cost of these lists varies, depending on the level of targeting sophistication. For example, a list of doctors working in the North East, specialising in orthopaedics will be more expensive than a list of men aged 18–26. Cost also depends on the usage of the list; it can be purchased for a one-off use, multiple use or unlimited use, during a pre-defined period. If you choose the latter, remember to request updates on the data to ensure that it remains as up to date as possible.

There are many ways to find the exact list that you need – visit www.marketinginspiration.com for some helpful advice and a list of resources.

Opinion leaders

This type of contact helps you by helping themself. Opinion leaders receive an associated benefit from using their personal reputation to promote your message. Their motivation for spreading a virus stems from the perception that they will:

- Achieve higher levels of self-respect
- End up with higher esteem in the eyes of others
- Feel good because they have helped someone else

Roughly between 20 per cent to 40 per cent of any target audience will have some kind of natural opinion leading effect. However, it is possible to identify and seed very powerful opinion leaders in your initial distribution list. These people are identified using personal knowledge and lateral thinking, however PR agencies may also offer a way to identify the opinion leaders for your market. For those without the luxury of a PR agency, a good place to start is to think about those individuals who hold most sway in your sector or whose opinions are most valued.

The supreme opinion leader

Given their position of authority and respect, journalists are uniquely powerful opinion leaders. It could be worth spending more effort targeting journalists because they have all the characteristics of a powerful opinion leader. In addition, they give you the opportunity to spread your viral idea through their publications to a very wide audience.

Locating journalists is a relatively easy job; they will always be credited in newspapers, websites and articles, as well as listed in media directories.

Existing customer database

It would be foolish to omit your existing customers from your initial distribution because these people already have a relationship with your organisation, provided they have given their permission to be contacted. Follow the normal targeting principles of selecting who is interested in your proposition.

Bear in mind, particularly if your customer database is especially large, that you will usually receive a more positive response if you identify people who have the characteristics listed below:

- Positive talkers – advocates who have probably already recommended you or your organisation
- Those who have had a positive experience with you
- Those who have volunteered information rather than been asked for it
- Those who have told you that they like what you do

Hewlett Packard talk to their customers

HP launched a successful business-to-business campaign through targeting existing customers with tailored news articles. Segmented by date of purchase and product, users received information on upgrades, maintenance and performance improvements, with a simple 'Recommend A Friend' option to encourage the viral effect.

The objective was to drive traffic to their website, and HP achieved a click-through rate in excess of 10 per cent from contacts from their own database. However, even these results were eclipsed by the click-through of up to 40 per cent for those recipients who had been referred by a friend or colleague, demonstrating the uplift created by a personal referral.

Five top tips for writing the perfect initial message
- Keep it short
- Avoid overt sales messages
- Let the audience discover the campaign for themselves
- Give a moving call to action
- Avoid corporate tone – keep it friendly and informal. Even make it look like a referral itself!

Indirect launch pads

Indirect launch pads offer an effective way to launch and sustain a viral marketing campaign. They work through the promotion of the campaign on shared interest 'third party' media, where communication is broadcast from one to many.

User groups/communities
User groups are online communities, based around chat platforms where individuals with a shared interest can interact with each other. As such, they offer an ideal seedbed for your viral campaign. Identify the user groups that contain the largest concentration of your audience and join in! (A simple Web search should go a long way to finding the user groups most relevant to your proposition.) Once you have joined the community, you can start to reference your campaign in discussions and forums, driving people towards

the content. Remember, however, to get your timing right and try not to be too overt or salesy. User groups exist for the benefit of the users and for them to share their opinions. They are not a marketing tool, so be careful not to alienate or annoy the community members.

For a great introduction to the world of the user group, visit www.geocities.com, which claimed 1.4 million members and 400,000 home pages in 2001, or www.tripod.com, with 1 million users and 1.6 million member-created pages. Others include Talk City, WBS, the Mining Company and the Globe.

Chatrooms
Outside the more formal user group environment, other popular chatrooms exist where it is easy for you to promote your viral content. Chatrooms appear on all sorts of websites. By thinking laterally about the habits of your user, you should be able to identify which chatrooms will offer the greatest exposure. Select only those chatrooms where users have a strong shared interest in your proposition, and – when the time is right (i.e. when the chatroom is busy) – make people aware of your campaign.

Message boards
Much like the informal chatroom, message boards offer a simple, albeit highly visible, opportunity to promote your content. Whereas chatrooms are active, real-time environments, message boards are more passive forums for interaction. Popular message boards offer a longer lasting method to increase awareness of your campaign.

Other marketing platforms
Remember that all communication platforms can form part of an indirect launch pad and serve to encourage the spread of

Buddy Lee for President

Lee Apparel successfully launched a viral marketing campaign to raise awareness of their dungaree products through message boards and chatrooms. The campaign featured the Buddy Lee doll – an icon from the 1960s – pushed as a presidential candidate. After a number of fake 'fan' sites were created, the marketing team used chatrooms to push 'Buddy For President' to create the impression that support was growing underground.

This clever launch technique underpinned a highly successful campaign, which saw 250,000 entries to a Buddy Lee competition and helped to fuel a sales increase of 125 per cent.

the virus through creating awareness and driving individuals to the content. Once exposed, these people may become part of the process, referring the virus themselves. There is no limit to which platforms can be used, from collateral and marketing material through to vehicle liveries. Remember your e-mail signature because it is so easy to change and can be very effective. Hotmail's famous example set the standard and Blue Mountain continue to use the technique, alerting every recipient of their e-greetings cards to their service through a strong e-mail sign off. Remember to integrate the customer touch points – it is important to consider viral marketing as an integral part of an overall marketing plan.

Your own Website
It may be obvious, but do not forget your own site when it comes to launching your virus. Promote your content on the

site, advertise it on your Home Page and make sure that when visitors come through to the viral content, the referral method is obvious. The most effective method is to include a 'recommend a friend' or 'e-mail this to a friend' button, which will encourage your visitors to participate in the viral effect.

Affiliate programs
Encourage your partners to include the virus on their website. This can be part of either a formal commercial agreement or a simple reciprocal arrangement. A button or text link will drive traffic through to your site, pulling users into the viral process.

Do not miss out on data collection

If you include a 'recommend a friend' button within your campaign, be sure to make the most of it. Do not limit the visitor to just one referral – give them the option to mail multiple contacts with your content, thereby increasing the spread. Also remember to take their details, so you can tell the recipient who referred the content to them if you are going to forward the content on their behalf.

Remember that data collection is important, but data protection regulations are more important. You cannot use the e-mail addresses of the people who have been referred content because they have not opted-in to your database. However, the sharpest marketers will have offered the visitor referring the content to their friends the ability to opt-in to future communication, thereby making his own data valid.

Timing

Once the campaign is live, it is impossible to control the timing (there is no way to regulate when a recipient will hit the forward button once a message is in their inbox). However, the timing of the initial distribution is easy to control for the direct launch pads. Moreover, the timing of this message can have a dramatic impact on the success of your campaign in making that all-important first referral.

Timing depends very much on the audience you are talking to. There are, however, certain broad rules to follow:

- Avoid Monday (especially Monday morning) as people are gearing up for the week
- Lunch-times are good – particularly if your target includes desk-bound professionals
- Avoid weekends for all campaigns – people have better things to do at this time than check their mail
- Friday afternoon is good because the working week reaches its most relaxed period.
- Avoid overnight distribution because spam (unsolicited e-mail) is usually sent out when servers are quiet. You do not want your campaign to be competing for attention against a load of junk e-mail

There is no substitute for experience, so try, try and try again. Watch the response carefully and see which times are gaining the highest response, then focus on this time for your future campaigns.

What happens when the campaign is launched?

People's propensity to forward a piece of content differs for each and every viral campaign. It depends on a number of environmental factors ranging from their mood and how busy they are, through to their position in society and affinity with your brand or proposition. That said, through our research we have identified four basic types of individual reaction to a viral campaign, outlined below.

- *Killer:* this person does not pass the message on, killing the virus there and then.
- *Selector:* this person will choose a small number of 'select' people to forward the message to – usually less than five.
- *Supporter:* a good person to know – this person will send the message on to between five and ten people.
- *Volumiser:* the ultimate recipient – this person will send the virus to more than 11 people.

Details from our research identified how these categories break down in terms of e-mail reaction:

Type of e-mail reaction	Percentage of respondents
Killer	2%
Selector	76%
Supporter	16%
Volumiser	6%

We all know volumisers – the person who seems to always send out the jokes or movie clips to a huge mailing list. While it may seem that these people are the ideal people to hit with a viral campaign, remember that volumisers can also have a negative effect on your campaign. We have mentioned the self-targeting nature of viral campaigns where recipients choose to pass the message on to contacts with a shared interest, thereby keeping the campaign broadly within the target market. We have also stressed the difference between targeted e-mail and spam; it is good to remember that even within a personal network, volumisers can be guilty of 'spamming' their friends and colleagues. People may receive your content from a volumiser, despite a lack of any shared interest in the content. This will create a 'killer' reaction when that recipient realises that they have been sent something in which they have no interest and therefore have no inclination to send on.

The death of your virus

Ultimately your virus will fizzle out and die. A time will come when the vast majority of interested people will have been infected and have forwarded it accordingly, or the campaign has failed to stimulate a strong referral process, limiting its exposure. Through natural fatigue, any virus will have to die sooner or later. The only thing a viral marketer can do is to use the launch pads we have discussed to maximise the life span of the campaign.

Summary

Today we have covered the different ways to launch and sustain a viral marketing campaign, and the importance of planning the timing of the initial distribution to maximise the chances of gaining the first referral. Tomorrow we shall look at how to track the performance of your campaign, and how

to turn this tracking information into tangible analysis.
Finally, we will recap what has been learnt this week,
creating a list of ten critical success factors.

Get going

By the end of today and the end of the week we will have:

- Recommended how you can measure your campaign
- Given advice on how to track and report on your campaign
- Summarised what we believe are the *critical success factors* for viral marketing campaigns

Over the last week you have covered a lot of content and been given much food for thought. Hopefully, along the way, you have been able to identify how a viral marketing campaign could work for you. Today we will look at the final element – the tracking and measurement of your virus to prove that your campaign has been a success. Following this we will take a brief review of the week, identifying ten critical success factors for viral marketing.

Measuring the immeasurable

In today's competitive business world, marketing needs to be measurable. Gone are the days when the advertising executive could famously state, *'I know half of my advertising budget is wasted, I just do not know which half'*. There is tremendous pressure to analyse all expenditure in order to ensure that it has been used in the most effective and efficient way possible.

Marketing in general and viral marketing in particular, are often perceived to be rather intangible – a murky world of costly campaigns without any real way to monitor Return on Investment (ROI). However, the reality is very different. Strong tracking and analysis has allowed marketers to demonstrate just what a fundamental return their campaigns can produce.

Campaign tracking

Tracking a viral campaign will vary according to the host environment – whether the campaign is hosted on a website or sent as an e-mail attachment. It is very simple to track visitor numbers to a website, whereas monitoring the spread of an e-mail is far more difficult – but not impossible!

For both options, the first step is to track the response of the initial launch. If you have used any direct launch pads this is quite simple – track the click-through to your initial e-mail. There are a number of companies who offer e-mail tracking such as E-circle, Expedite or Responsys, or your agency may use some bespoke software, however, you should be able to check the performance of the initial direct launch.

Once the user-to-user referral process begins, the tracking methods are different for the two host options. For campaigns based on e-mail, tracking is usually lost at this point, but there is one way to gain a small insight into how far the virus has spread. By including in the e-mail itself, a transparent graphic file which is hosted on a website, you will be able to measure how often the e-mail is opened and by how many unique users. This works each time the e-mail is opened by a user

who is connected to the internet – a request is sent by the computer to the website for the Web-hosted graphic file (please note this does not apply to all platforms, for example cable access e-mail does not support this). Once the request is received, the image is sent back down to the user. All this can happen without the user even knowing their computer had requested a Web-hosted graphic, providing the viral marketer with all the information they need to run analysis on the tracking information collected.

While both legal and perfectly ethical, it must be stated that this method of tracking is not totally accurate. Users viewing the content offline will not be counted in the overall figures because no request for the Web-hosted graphic can be made. That said, this process does give the viral marketer a rough measure of the overall usage of the campaign.

Rather more detail can be gained from Web-hosted content, simply through using any of the many Web usage monitoring software packages. These packages, such as Web Trends, will look at the log files which record usage of a site and create useful, concise reports showing a whole raft of information which is useful in its own right. Typically the report will show:

- Number of unique users (i.e. not the same users coming back for a repeat visit)
- Number of new versus returning users
- Where groups of users came from – both geographically and digitally (where they were referred from)
- How long users typically used the site for
- At what point users left the site
- What the most active time periods were (by day and time period)

Even better than these static reports are 'live' reporting tools, which offer real-time reports on exactly who is on your site. These packages, such as Live Stats from Media House Software can often be downloaded; sometimes they are even free of charge for a trial period and they can give amazing insight into how the campaign is performing. As well as providing the basic reports detailed above, live reports allow you to feel the excitement of the campaign; you can see 'real' people coming on to the site to view your content.

For any reporting tool to work, you will need to have access to the log files from the Web server – these should be available, but remember to ask for them up front. If they are not saved they cannot be recreated and you will lose valuable information. If you are working with an IT colleague or agency, make sure they know that you need to run reports on the site usage.

For more information on the reporting tools and links to places where they are available for free download or trial, visit www.marketinginspiration.com.

Turning statistics into information – the analysis and ROI measures

With the statistics you have gleaned from the campaign tracking, you will already have the raw information to show how successful the campaign has been. Although this offers some insight into the performance of the campaign, calculating a real return on the investment is a great way to put flesh on these bones. The simplest and most effective way to calculate a return is to consider the investment and results in terms of equivalent marketing spend. Take a look at the example below.

Let us say that your campaign website had 50,000 hits and cost £10,000. Firstly your cost per hit is 20p. Next think how many page impressions on banner advertising you would have needed to generate the same 50,000 hits. Presuming an optimistic 2 per cent click-through means you would have needed 2,500,000 banner impressions. At a rough cost of £100 per thousand, you would have paid £250,000 for those same 50,000 hits. So this rough comparison of effectiveness gives a ratio of 1:25 – in other words your spend on viral marketing has been 25 times more effective than online advertising media spend.

Whilst this comparison method is by no means 100 per cent accurate, it does give an insight into the overall effectiveness of the campaign, which is the best basis for deciding on how the marketing budget should be split.

A more tangible measurement is data capture. The data you collect can be used to give valuable insights into who your customers are, what they do, their likes and dislikes. It also boosts the size of the company's database, ready to improve the effectiveness of future marketing initiatives.

What data to collect?

The data you collect has two elements: Who and What.

The **Who** element is simple, standard information detailing who that person is: name, sex, address, postcode, e-mail address, telephone and mobile number. This information allows you to recognise the individual.

The **What** element adds insight into what that person is like. Here it is important to get the information you need. This could be simple information like age or marital status, or in a business-to-business context, job title or area of responsibility. If, for example, your target market is golfers, remember to ask if that person has a handicap or is a member of a club. This information will help you to build up a profile of the individual. Once segmented, it is easier to tailor communications to a segment's specific requirements.

Ten critical success factors

Over the last week you have looked at all the key features of a successful viral marketing campaign. We shall now review

the key points made during the week, producing ten critical
success factors of a viral marketing campaign.

Understand your audience
The success of a viral marketing initiative is less to do with
those who orchestrate it, and everything to do with the target
audience. Identifying and understanding them is essential.
Audience-centric planning will help guarantee that the end
user is kept at the forefront of your mind. Understanding the
audience will drive the entire campaign, from the initial idea,
message, chosen characteristic and vehicle, to the timing and
creative execution.

It starts with a good, simple idea
This primarily refers to the content of your message,
although simplicity is key throughout the execution. You
need to ensure that the message is as potent further down the
line as it is for the first recipient. Make sure that everyone can
understand it consistently.

Exploit human behaviour
Consider what consumers like and apply this to your target
audience. Would the campaign idea pass the 'What's in it for
me?' test.

Remember your initial objectives and reflect these throughout
– are you generating sales with an offer or are you building
awareness with a brand message? Make sure you select the
most appropriate vehicles and characteristics to do the job.

And finally, remember what annoys people – reconsider the
research results mentioned on Wednesday in order to
understand people's propensity to become infected with the
virus.

Keep it open

The more complex the execution, the greater the chance that
it will not work. Understand your audience and create a
campaign that fits their profile. Do not fall into the trap of
choosing the lowest common denominator because this will
compromise the creative execution. Rather, aim for a balance
between technical innovation and access. Remember that the
easier and smoother it is for your audience to experience
your content, the more likely they are to send it on.

Make sure it scales

If your viral campaign features Web-hosted content, make
sure that your technical platform is up to the job. A
successful campaign will place an increased burden on your
IT architecture and, if this fails, the campaign will fail too.
Talk to your technical people and your service provider or
hosting partner to make sure that the systems in place can
handle the volume of traffic that you are hoping for.

There is more than one way to catch a virus

When launching or sustaining your viral campaign, you have
more than one option. Consider the balance and mix between
direct and indirect launch pads, for example, e-mailing your
closest friends and family or customer database, while
penetrating user groups and exploiting your own website.

Integrate the touch points

It is unlikely that your viral campaign will work in isolation;
integrating both your marketing strategy and other
marketing activities is crucial. Give people the same
customer experience in your virus as they would expect
elsewhere – both in terms of the message you are trying to
convey and the creative execution.

Keep both eyes on the results

You can track your campaign by using some specific technologies arguably, however, final analysis is actually more important. Use the techniques mentioned earlier today to turn statistics into ROI information. Learn from your successes and your failures, and do not forget that some results will be instant, some will be delayed.

Get the right team involved

Like all marketing initiatives you need the right people on board – engage with your Web team and technical people, talk to your product specialists and choose your marketing or new media agency wisely. Visit www.marketinginspiration.com for some helpful guidance and an agency resource centre.

Be committed, single-minded and have some fun

Your commitment to viral marketing is an essential factor. Too often marketers avoid viral campaigns because of a mythical fear factor or because of a misguided view that viral marketing cannot work for them. The key is to give it a go – commit to a simple test campaign and see it through – you may be amazed by the results.

A first attempt at viral marketing does not have to be the most sophisticated campaign ever produced. You do not need six figure budgets. All you need is a good idea and the knowledge you have learnt over the last 7 days.

Final thoughts

Viral marketing has been praised and criticised more than any other medium in recent times. Nevertheless, the

potential returns speak for themselves and the mediu.
here to stay. So, when planning your next marketing
campaign, keep the following points in mind.

- Which marketing medium makes every participant a brand advocate?
- Which is the most user-friendly type of marketing?
- Which marketing vehicle is delivered with immediate credibility?
- Which marketing tool quantifiably improves the efficiency of marketing spend and ROI?

The answer is clear to us – viral marketing is an essential part of the 21st century communication mix.

SUN

MON

TUE

WED

THU

FRI

SAT

For information

on other

IN A WEEK titles

go to

www.inaweek.co.uk